"REINVENTION IS THE RESULT OF THE UNIVERSE GIVING US THE NECESSITY FOR CHANGE."

—MARY ANN FAREMOUTH

REVOLUTIONARY REINVENTION WORKBOOK

HOW TO REDISCOVER YOUR SKILLS AND PASSIONS AND REINVENT YOUR CAREER

MARY ANN FAREMOUTH

NORTH STAR ATHENA
PUBLISHING LLC

Published by North Star Athena Publishing LLC, Houston, Texas

For more info, please visit www.faremouth.com, or email the author at faremouth@sbcglobal.net.

Content/Developmental Editing by Max Regan
Line Editing / Proofreading by Marva Mason
Cover Design and Book Layout by MarkGelotte.com

ISBN-978-0-9988658-8-1

Dedicated to my grandmother Mimi

and to our conversations that offered me

both hope and wisdom.

CONTENTS

INTRODUCTION IX
It's Time to Rediscover Your Career IX
Reinventing Your Work With the New Work World IX
A Guide for the Path Forward X
The Faremouth Method X
Slaying the Fear Dragon XI
Activate Your Journal XI
The World Needs Your Gifts XII

Chapter 1
DOING A SELF-INVENTORY 1
Finding Your Core Values and Belief 3
Times When You Have Been FORCED to Grow and Change 5
Experience With Self-Assessment Tests 7
Asking for Help and Guidance: Who Do You Turn To and Why? 8
Parts of Yourself You Are Most Proud Of 9
Your History of Work 10
Discovering Your Strengths and Obstacles 13
What You Loved and Hated About Your Last Job 14
Goal Setting: Your Current Career Search 15
Relationship Building/Community/Networking 17
Lesson Learned From Difficulty and Ease 18
Finding Alignment 21

Chapter 2
ASKING BETTER QUESTIONS 22
Staying True to Yourself 22
Using Questions to Create Clarity 25
Starting Over 27
The Effects of Our Choices on Others 28
Building a Better Future 31

Chapter 3
STEPPING OUT OF YOUR COMFORT ZONE....35
The Starting Place 36
Strengthening Your Imagination.... 37
Storms, Roadblocks and Failure 40
Exploring Your Relationship With Fear 42
Times When You Have Been FORCED To Adapt and Change 43
Calculated Risk....44
A New Mindset: Review, Reconsider, Restart.... 45
Coming Home to Who You Really Are.... 48

Chapter 4
TAKING THE TIME TO DO IT RIGHT.... 49
Taking Your Time 49
Rushing Through It 51
Planning and Goal Setting 52
Training Towards Excellence.... 55
Getting the Support We Need to Succeed 56

Chapter 5
BE A HUNTER 58
The Hunter's Mindset.... 59
Being a Leader 62
Moving Past Failure and Fear 63
Deciding What Is Most Necessary.... 65
Making Decisions and Going for It.... 66
Embracing Innovation 67
Searching for More 70
Using the Campfire 72
How We Win Matters 74

Chapter 6
CONCLUSION: THE HUMAN ELEMENT....76
Rediscovering Your Answers/Rediscovering Yourself.... 76
A Vision to Move Towards 78
Living Your Truth 79
Putting It Into Action 80
Checklist for Getting Ready for Your Next Job.... 81
The Human Element and the Importance of Giving Back 83
Simple Steps With Profound Results 85
A New Mindset for the New Work World 86
Coming Home 87
ACKNOWLEDGMENTS 89
REFERENCES 90
ABOUT MARY ANN FAREMOUTH....91

INTRODUCTION

IT'S TIME TO REDISCOVER YOUR CAREER

In early 2020 we all experienced a global health crisis on a scale that the modern world has never seen. In the United States jobless numbers and unemployment rates skyrocketed and many folks worked to move their careers online. The world is forever changed. This pandemic stopped many of us in our tracks in our personal and professional lives and forced us all to do some very serious thinking about where we go from here.

As we navigate this crisis, protecting ourselves and those we love and care for, it is hard to imagine that life will ever "get back to normal" and yet, at some point we will. Of course, in the job and hiring markets there will be a "new normal" that job seekers must be aware of if they want to stay competitive and re-start or re-craft their careers. That is why this book was written with the intent to help job seekers uncover the full range of their skills, interests, and passions so they can rediscover and remake their careers. It is now our job, our mission, to find ways to REINVENT ourselves using revolutionary techniques that lead to real results.

What if you could learn to navigate these changes in a way that gives you joy and purpose and expands your ability to contribute to the greater good? What if there was a tried and true proven method that could provide a systematic way to get into this alignment? Would that make the process easier?

Reinventing Your Career in The New Work World

The word "Reinvention" means the action or process through which something is changed so much that it appears to be entirely new. The willingness to embrace reinvention can be an exciting time of self-discovery. There may be hidden talents and passions that you have pushed to the background for one reason or another. Now you have an opportunity for discovery and reawakening what has been deeply buried within yourself. Reinvention is all about getting into appropriate alignment or relative position to the SELF. The Self, most specifically, as it relates to your own skills and passions and to the New Work World.

In these Revolutionary times many of us are feeling out of sync in some way, shape or form with the self. We do not know who we are, what is really happening, and where we are going. This book is going to take you by the hand, gently, and guide you through a series of exercises to help you get into alignment with yourself, and allow you to experience more happiness, fulfillment and purpose.

For many of us this will be a Revolutionary Reinvention. It will require us to examine our own life experiences with employment and work and to articulate our deepest values, so that we can stay connected to doing the work that will fulfill us the most.

A Guide for the Path Forward

I have been a professional recruiter and consultant for over 30 years, and I am always amazed how many people are in the wrong job. Is your job and career in sync with who you truly are? In my first book, *Revolutionary Recruiting*, I shared stories of those whose job threatened their happiness, their relationships and even their lives. This historical moment we are all in has called us to stop in our tracks and take stock of many aspects of our lives and to make decisions about how we want to go forward. To do that effectively, you must be able to see what skills you really do have and how they can be highlighted or transferred into a new career or job. This book and the exercises in it will walk you through the process and allow you to be more aware to make those choices.

The Faremouth Method

The Faremouth Method is a series of five tried and proven stages that can be used by job seekers, employers, and recruiters to assess their passion with their purpose in making the right match between people and positions.

These steps can also assist you in going through the process of getting into alignment and hopefully allow you to gather important information about yourself and your skill set going forward. The steps can be used to assist you in achieving any goal.

The basics steps are:

Do A Self Inventory

Ask Better Questions

Step Out of Your Comfort Zone

Take the Time to Do It Right

Be a Hunter

Slaying the Fear Dragon

As a recruiter I have used this method to get candidates into alignment with their skill set to be able to make a career change. In working with people in their quest to improve their career, I would find that FEAR is often the big dragon within that holds so many of us back from moving forward with taking on new challenges. The Faremouth Method is like having five powerful swords folded into one, a tool that gives us the ability to slay that ugly dragon of fear and self-doubt. Right now, we are each on our own personal and professional quest to slay that dragon within that might be holding us back from moving forward and getting on track in life.

When seeking the perfect job fit, we do a self-inventory, ask better questions, step out of our comfort zone, take our time to do it right and learn how to be a "hunter." These are the steps that lead to a more sustainable career path. By engaging with this workbook, carefully considering, and answering each of these questions chapter by chapter will help you gather the vital information that can make all the difference. In this book we will use questions and insights from The Faremouth Method as well as the system that I use when consulting with individual employers and job seekers. These steps assess your current or recent job; your background and training; your passions, skills and interests; the documents and tools that allow others to connect with you and your willingness to reshape your career to meet the opportunities and challenges of this new world we are stepping into together. In this workbook these systems will be used to bring you the questions and answers you need to find out who you really are and what job or career would be the best fit for you.

Activate Your Journal

This workbook has questions, opportunities, and exercises on every page. You might choose to write in the workbook, or you might prefer to keep your own journal or notebook where you can track and record your answers. If you choose to keep a journal while you use this workbook then ACTIVATE it! Make lists, tell stories, sketch, or doodle, and allow your creativity to come forward. Remember, no one is going to see this workbook or journal except YOU and the key is to feel free to answer each question fully and honestly so you can gather the insight and information that will serve you the most! This workbook is a vehicle to help you with this process and allow you to investigate how YOU can REINVENT yourself with these Revolutionary changes and enjoy your personal and professional work life to the fullest. Let's get started!

The World Needs Your Gifts

This global pandemic has reminded many of us of how fragile life can be and how vital it is to live our lives to the fullest. How do we do that? How do we take stock of our own personal and professional gifts and reinvent ourselves to discover a job and career that is meaningful, fulfilling and has purpose? We need and deserve jobs that give us joy and allow us to come home to our families and friends as happy and healthy as possible. This will require us to dig in with honesty, flexibility, and strategy so we can create the work lives that we have been waiting for.

Revolutionary times require revolutionary action. Everything has changed from the interview process to how our jobs are performed in this New Work World. We are all having to adapt to an even more technologically driven career. We are now having to conduct the interview process online; learn how we can work remotely and how we can become more competitive and in demand by reinventing our skill set as we seek new employment. We are all in the process of assessing ourselves through an honest and deep path of discovery of who we truly are and what we have to offer.

Enjoy!

Mary Ann Faremouth
Houston TX

CHAPTER 1

DOING A SELF-INVENTORY

Have you ever had an experience that really made you stop in your tracks and think? I am talking about a profound experience that became embedded in your mind. I had such an experience in the summer of 2009 when I visited the Temple of Apollo at Delphi in Greece.

The porous stone and limestone remains of the Temple sit along the rugged slopes of the Parnassos Mountains. It was a magical experience to capture the Temple's magnificence, not only in sight but also in its aura. The tall, aged stone columns reached high into the sky as I looked up and saw the inscription in Greek, "Know Thyself." I knew that there must be a reason that inscription has lasted all these years while other parts of the temple have deteriorated. I realized that the philosophers and scholars in the 7th Century B.C. knew something very profound and that the message still stands the test of time. Fulfillment in life is all about "Knowing Thyself." From that trip to Delphi, the First Step of The Faremouth Method was born.

This first step in the process is, in many ways, the most crucial because "Knowing Thyself" is truly what allows you to achieve great things. After all, aligning your work life and your career with who you truly are, begins with KNOWING who you truly are. We all know life can throw us curve balls that sometimes catch us off guard. Those challenges can also make our core personalities, values, passions, and beliefs expand and grow. Understanding and feeling confident about the core of who we are, once it becomes solid, usually allows us to become unshakable. Confucius said, "Choose a job you love, and you will never have to work a day in your life." In other words, if we are aligned with a career path that fits with who we are, work just might seem effortless and enjoyable!

But what do you do if you feel lost and not sure of what that core even IS anymore? Who are you really? Have you changed? What do you truly value and want from your career and your life? You can always take self-assessment tests, go to counseling, work with a coach or a spiritual guide or your priest or minister, but you yourself have a great capacity to take a self-inventory and discover what you value in your life and in your work. No matter how different or unique you might feel, it is vital that you feel confident in who you are and what interests and motivates you.

There is an expanding world of technical and vocational trade schools now on the rise due to finances, time constraints, passion, and interest. There are a number of young people coming out of high school who have no desire to attend universities or obtain a degree. Trade schools focus upon short term programs such as culinary schools, welding, aesthetician, hair stylist, medical tech, cabinetry and woodworking, plumbing, and many other skilled categories. There are numerous IT creative programs that fall under this category such as web design and programming.

The following exercises are designed to get you more in line with this CORE self, to find out what you value and what matters most to you in your work and career.

Finding Your Core Values and Beliefs

1. List the five most important qualities that you find in yourself. Are you creative? Confident? Loyal? Intelligent?
   -
   -
   -
   -
   -

2. Now RANK that list you just made, which qualities are the strongest? Put those at the top of the list.
   -
   -
   -
   -
   -

3. Make a list of your greatest skills. What are you terrific at? Problem solving? Innovating? Telling the truth?
   -
   -
   -

4. Make a list of what qualities OTHER PEOPLE have praised in you or your work. Have coaches or teachers or bosses or co-workers told you that you excel at something? What was it?

   ______________________told me I was good at ________________________

   ______________________told me I was good at ________________________

   ______________________told me I was good at ________________________

5. Which qualities do you value most in your colleagues, your co-workers or bosses? Clear communication? No-Drama? Honesty? Trust?

Times When You Have Been FORCED to Grow and Change

1. Make a list of five unexpected events in your family or personal life that affected you personally; some type of adversity you had to overcome? What did you have to survive? The death of a family member? An illness? A change in school or career? A heartbreak? Be as specific as you can.

    -
    -
    -
    -
    -

2. Choose one of those events in the list above and describe it in detail. What happened?

3. What lessons did you learn from this survival? How did you grow or change as a person?

Experience with Self-Assessment Tests

1. Have you ever taken a formal self-assessment test or used a self-assessment tool? What type of tool was it? A personality test? The Myers-Briggs test? DiSC Assessment? Describe what you learned from the test if anything.

2. Have you ever used an informal tool for assessing your personality or your strengths and weaknesses? What was it? The Enneagram Personality Test? Astrology? IQ testing? Describe what these tools taught you about yourself if anything.

3. What are three hard truths you learned about yourself in your last job or two?
   -
   -
   -

Asking for Help and Guidance: Who Do You Turn To and Why?

1. Who are some of the people you have turned to in your life when you have needed help or advice, especially about your career path. Siblings? Co-workers? Coaches? Teachers?

2. What is the best career advice you ever received, general or specific, and who gave it to you?

3. Name two people in your life who truly understand your career goals and why they matter to you.
   -
   -

4. Name three people in any area of your life who you feel have your back, no matter what.
   -
   -
   -

Parts of Yourself You Are Most Proud Of

1. Name three things you have achieved in your work life that you are the proudest of, even if they are things you might never brag to others about.
    -
    -
    -

2. Describe a time you helped or supported a friend, relative, colleague or co-worker. Who did you help? How did you help? Did helping them change you in any way or teach you anything?

Your History of Work

Understanding your own history in the workforce is vital when seeking to align yourself more fully with who you truly are and what you truly want to do. After all, our "work" in the world means many things over the course of our lives, not just our formal training or career. The best gifts in life are not always wrapped in pretty little boxes with elaborate bows on top. They are sometimes in the form of challenging experiences and/or failures that teach us valuable lessons. Lessons that have lifelong marks on our character and future endeavors. In the workplace, at some point in our lives, we have had our share of good experiences and bad. We have had jobs we hated and jobs we loved. We have had bosses that we enjoyed working for and those we want to just forget. Through it all, lessons were learned along the journey, and growth and development happened along the way. Let's examine some of these job experiences that might give us insight into who we are today and even more importantly, where we want to go.

1. What was your first unpaid job? Taking care of a sibling? Carrying the groceries in from the car? Cleaning the house? Describe that job or responsibility here.

2. What was your first paid job? Describe where you worked, how old you were, what your responsibilities were, if you liked it, who you worked with, how long it lasted, etc.

3. What messages did you get from parents or teachers or other adults about finding your career or your "work" in the world? Were you taught that work was a necessary evil? Were you taught your job could be fun? Were you taught that your career should pay you well? What messages or values influenced you the most and whom did those messages come from?

4. What was your WORST job, paid or unpaid, at any age? What did you hate about it and why? How did you leave? What were you doing? Imagine three things that COULD have happened but did not (no matter how wildly you must imagine!) that would have made that job more bearable.

5. What was your BEST job, paid or unpaid? Did you get paid? Did you intern? Volunteer?
   What were the ingredients of your most favored job so far?

Discovering Your Strengths and Obstacles

1. Name three things that have always come easily to you in your job or career. Are you always on time? Do you always get along with others?

    -
    -
    -

2. Name three specific things you have struggled with in your jobs or career. Have you had trouble with authority? Have you been bored or not challenged enough? Have you wanted greater opportunities for advancement? Have you been unsatisfied with your salary?

    -
    -
    -

What You Loved and Hated About Your Last Job

1. Think of your most recent job. What worked about that job? What did not?

2. If you could have changed one thing about the job what would it have been?

3. There are always tasks that we like more than others in any job. Maybe you do not like to do tedious work and would rather engage in conversation with clients. What tasks did you start out hating in that job but then began to like and why?
   -
   -
   -

4. What tasks did you dislike and KEPT disliking?
   -
   -
   -

5. What tasks have you done in that job that may have gotten you positive attention or recognition? What tasks or experiences have gotten you negative attention?

Goal Setting: Your Current Career Search

Goal setting is such an important ingredient in accomplishing positive improvements. I have often heard if you really want to accomplish a goal you need to WRITE IT DOWN AND PUT A DATE BY IT. Many variables, especially these days, can play into accomplishing our goals. Let's consider important goals you might have and the steps we might have to take to achieve them.

1. What is your crazy wild dream job? Its ok if its wildly unrealistic. Describe it in detail, even if it is a fantasy!

2. What is your realistic dream job or position that you feel IS within the realm of possibility? What is the job title, responsibilities, salary line, benefits?

3. What are your five most important short-term or long-term goals right now? Put a check mark next to those you feel most achievable or realistic.

    •

    •

    •

    •

    •

4. Have you taken any steps towards those goals? What were they?

Relationship Building/Community/Networking

Life is really all about relationships. If this global pandemic is teaching us anything, it is that relationships are vital. As human beings we need contacts to continue to grow personally as well as professionally. There are many ways to accomplish this task.

1. What are the important relationships or culture fits that you would consider most vital in your ideal workplace?

2. Have you done work to strengthen a community or group within your job or career or worked to cultivate more professional contacts? Have you attended any networking functions? Made more personal contacts?

3. Have you joined any on-line learning or training programs to strengthen or diversify your skills? What have you done and how did it help?

4. Much of this recent period of social distancing has kept us away from in-person workplaces, team events and office spaces. What have you missed most by not having regular contact with peers and co-workers?

Lessons Learned From Difficulty and Ease

1. I remember my first job when I was 16 years old. It was the job where I worked for one the toughest bosses ever. He was dictatorial, no-nonsense, had very high standards, and he was my Dad. He owned a restaurant that was very popular among automotive workers in a very blue-collar town. He opened at 4:30 a.m. every morning. Working for him taught me a few of the most valuable lessons in my career. I learned that having good customer service skills allowed me to make good tips. I learned that rising early was taxing but it allowed me to have much of the afternoon to myself. I learned that perseverance pays off and that striving to be the best you can be allows you to have high standards in your life. I learned how to listen and that making mistakes would not kill me.

   Who was your most difficult or toughest boss and what lessons did you learn from them?

2. Later in my career I had a boss who was probably the nicest man I ever worked for. Mr. Jones was the Director of an Engineering department of a Big Three automaker. He knew I was going to college in the evening when I worked for him. He had worked and gone to school himself to get his degree, so he was very accommodating with me coming in late and leaving early, using downtimes to study, and often taking half days off on Friday. Having a boss so positive all the time allowed me to believe in myself more.

   Who was the nicest boss you ever worked for and what did you learn from them, positive or negative?

3. Lots of people are feeling OUT of Alignment these days. What are the parts of your work or home life that feel the most out of alignment?

4. If you have recently lost your job, been furloughed, or laid off, how did that make you feel? Name and describe some of those feelings here.

5. If you are working from home, does that feel less productive or alienating for you? What are some of the struggles you have faced in working remotely?

6. What are the best or easiest parts about working remotely?

7. Are you feeling supported by your family environment? If not, what might make it easier or better?

8. Are there specific ways that you have noticed stress or anxiety showing up around your job or career lately? If you have had a specific experience of fear or stress or feeling overwhelmed or uncertainty, describe it here.

9. How have these factors affected or strengthened your personal relationships with family, friends, or co-workers?

10. Have recent financial burdens or changes changed your life significantly? If so how?

Finding Alignment

1. What would being "IN Alignment" look like to you these days?

2. Would having the same job or working in your same field be a comfort or a consternation to you?

3. What would a "Happy Self" look like right now? Are mindfulness practices helpful to you at all?

4. List four simple, healthy steps you could take this week, even if super small, to move in the direction with the job and career you want.

    -
    -
    -
    -

The answers you discovered to all these questions are the first vital step in The Faremouth Method, so keep this information close at hand. It will provide you with insight and awareness about what you have been through, what you have learned, what you want and what you really value.

CHAPTER 2

ASKING BETTER QUESTIONS

After we do a Self-Inventory, it's time to begin asking deeper questions that are not just about who we have been, but ones designed to bring us insight about who we are becoming and who we want to be. Asking ourselves these tough questions allow us to live our truth in ways that will uplift every aspect of our lives. As we prepare for this new journey, we find that by asking better questions will give you the time to prepare honest responses to ensure better results as well as educate yourself to secure a better job offer in the future.

Asking ourselves better questions allow us to plan out a more methodical roadmap to get us where we need to go. It can help us keep our career goal front and center and budget the resources and time it will take to achieve.

Staying True to Yourself

We make a lot of choices and compromises over the course of our work lives and careers. Sometimes we take a job we do not like because the salary is too good to pass up. We find temporary work to bridge the gap until our dream job materializes. We let opportunities go by because we are unsure of what we really want or if risks are worth taking. The key purpose of self-discovery is to find what is most TRUE about yourself; what you really want, believe, value and trust. Then we can make better career choices that let us Stay True to what we know about ourselves.

1. What ideas or people do you value the most in all the world? Rank in order of importance:
   -
   -
   -
   -
   -
   -
   -
   -

2. What abstract concepts are most vital to you? Which ones would you sacrifice or die for? Freedom? Justice? Fairness? Financial? Family?
   -
   -
   -
   -
   -

3. Choose one of the words on your list above and write about it for a moment. What does family mean to you? Or freedom?

4. Describe a time when you felt that you were really being true to who you were in your personal and professional life? Where were you? When was it? What happened?

Using Questions to Create Clarity

Questions and answers have always been used to help individuals gather information that brings more clarity in aligning your true self with your career goals.

1. At this point in your career, do you feel that you have the correct skill set, education, and experience to get where you want to go? Have you considered online courses to receive training, degrees or certifications that would make you more marketable? List a few of the things you could do to increase, broaden, or expand your ability, education, or skill set:
   -
   -
   -
   -
   -

2. If you did want to train in new areas or study something new, how might you find the time and resource to pay for that new training? What would you be willing to do or not do? Hire outside help to take care of kids or help with household duties? Would you be willing to take a part-time or evening job? Would you severely curtail your free/social time and use that time to study or work longer hours?

3. If finances are tight in general and you are trying to shift your career, what things would you be willing to do or not do to bring in more money, even if it was temporary? Would you put forth more effort in your current job, take on more responsibilities or work more hours? Would you be willing to learn additional skills to become promoted?

- I would be willing to
- I would be willing to
- I would be willing to
- I would be willing to
- I would NOT be willing to
- I would NOT be willing to
- I would NOT be willing to
- I would NOT be willing to

4. The word "Holistic" simply means taking the WHOLE person into consideration. It is a mindset in which we do not divide ourselves into separate parts with career over here, health over there, family over there, money over there. Instead we consider ourselves to be one, whole, integrated individual. A holistic approach means looking at the whole person, seeing our financial, relational, physical, emotional, and spiritual wellbeing as all deeply interconnected.
   What would it mean to you being a more "holistic" employee or having a more "holistic" career?

Starting Over

We "start over" a million times over the course of our lives. Every day when we wake up and head to work, every new year and every birthday, each new job or relationship, every new school we attend or town we live in, all mark new beginnings. You have probably started over (and over) in your own life more times than you can count. Understanding this process will help you when seeking to restart or re-align your job and your career path.

1. What is your first memory of a time in your life when you feel you had to "start over" or "begin again"? Where were you? How old? When was it? What happened?

2. Was starting over easy? Difficult? Did anyone help or support you?

3. What holds you back from the feeling you could start over in your career? What are the fears that arise? Do you feel you are too old to start over or that you do not have the money or time?

4. Are you ever concerned about what family/peers/loved ones would say if you took your work life in a new direction? Who is in your world who might approve or not approve?

The Effects of Our Choices on Others

We live in communities, circles and families, and our relationships are central to how we define our lives. This means that the decisions and changes we make in our work lives impact the lives of others as well. That is why it is important to look carefully at who supports our work lives and who will be most affected if our work world changes.

Sometimes when we articulate our truth and our real values and goals and begin to act on them, we risk losing those whose vision of who we are and can be is more limited than our own. Answering these questions will bring answers and not everyone will agree with the answers you find. This can cause conflict, but it might also be a great opportunity to move away from those who hold you back. Finding our own answers can also be a way to learn that we will not always please everyone. It can make us open to new connections, new opportunities, and new friendships with those who share our strong and clear energy for who we are becoming and who we already are!

1. Who was the first person who ever really believed in your strengths and abilities in the work world? How did you know that person? Were they a parent? Teacher? Coach? Old boss? Mentor? Friend?

2. What message did they give you about your skills or strengths?

3. What are the top biggest fears you hold these days about how your changing work life might negatively impact the people closest to you?
   -
   -
   -
   -

4. If you were happier and more fulfilled in your career what are some of the specific positive benefits that might impact the people closest to you?
   -
   -
   -
   -
   -

5. Are there people who you feel hold you back or who constantly doubt or question or criticize you, especially in the way you manage your work life and career? How do you handle this when it happens?
   -
   -
   -

6. Currently in your life whose opinions are most important to you? Family? Bosses? Parents? Strangers?
   -
   -
   -
   -

7. What are some of the things you do or have done to please or impress others in your work world?

8. Are you open to making new friends and developing new peer relationships? What qualities would you most value in a new friend, peer, or co-worker?

Building a Better Future

The future starts right now. Not tomorrow or next week. We are building our future and moving towards it, shaping it, with every choice we make. Often by asking ourselves better questions we can create more clarity with our future vision and goals. Our future can become more clear and not so fuzzy if we know the steps we must take to get to where we need and want to go.

1. What is the ideal future you would like to see for yourself in the next five years in your life and work world? What does that job or life or home or business or career look like exactly? Describe it here:

2. If you have your Dream Career or Dream Job firmly in your mind, what changes, real or imagined, would you have to make to get to where you want to go in your work life? What would have to change?
    -
    -
    -
    -
    -

3. How could you fit into that future being in more alignment with who you are today?

4. Often the trick to building a more solid future in our career is to transform the word "WHY" into the words "WHY NOT."

Make five statements about your work life framed as questions using the word "why." For example, "Why doesn't my boss appreciate me more?" or "Why did they get a promotion instead of me?"

-
-
-
-
-

5. Now try writing those same five questions with the words "why not." For example, "Why not ask my boss what else I could do to improve my next performance review?" or "Why not ask the gal who got the promotion to tell me more about the advanced training program she took last year so I can decide if it might be useful for me in improving my own promotability?"
   -
   -
   -
   -
   -

6. Building our own future is often fueled by supporting others in building theirs. Are you being a Mentor or Friend to a co-worker, family member or associate who might also be going through a similar experience? Who could you reach out to and offer your support?
   -
   -
   -

7. There are parts of the future we have within our own control and parts we do not. Understanding this can ease a great deal of strain and anxiety as we build our future. What are three parts of your world you have control over? Where you live? What jobs you apply for? How you present yourself professionally?
   -
   -
   -

8. What are three parts you do NOT have control over? Politics? Health crisis? What your co-workers decide to do?
   -
   -
   -

9. If you are a very social person, and the ideal job you would like is now one that may require you to work from home, how could you have a sense of community around you without being with others in an office?

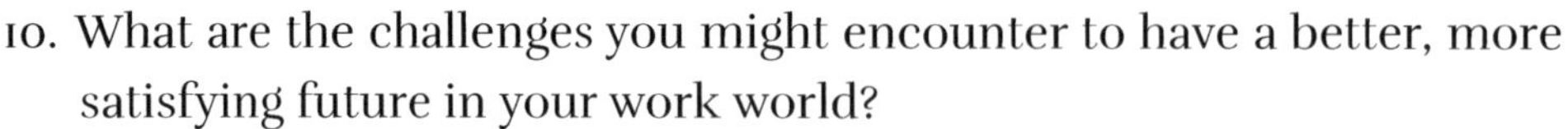

10. What are the challenges you might encounter to have a better, more satisfying future in your work world?

The above answers are the second step in this process of learning to ask better questions in your job search. They are providing you with more information of discernment as you undergo your study of awareness of where you have come from and where you are going. You are getting a better idea of how you might fit in certain jobs that you may not have realized before.

CHAPTER 3

STEPPING OUT OF YOUR COMFORT ZONE

With all the changes going on in our lives and especially as we move together into the New Work World, I am reminded of a quote by Wayne Dyer, "If you change the way you look at things, things you look at change." He was so right. And Neale Donald Walsch famously said, "Life begins at the end of our comfort zone." He was right too!

When you change the way you see the world, when your intentions are positive and powerful, when you search for the good in a situation, then you can transform your life into the amazing journey and adventure it was designed to be. Even in this time in history of unique crisis and lots of unknowns, we can still change our mindset and that is the change than can empower us the most.

We have to put forth a conscious and deliberate effort to change how we think in order to create our own new reality and this requires us to step out of our comfort zone, to shift our regular ways of doing things. Does staying in a safe and easy job or relationship that does not feel "like home" really allow a person to grow and expand?

When we imagine what that New Work World might look like for us, then we are then able to see ourselves in a much better position where we can thrive economically and personally. This is where we can move our own personal mountains and envision what is on the other side of our current reality, in order for us to become more productive and deliberate individuals.

The Starting Place

1. How would you describe your "Comfort Zone" in your career so far? Where have you been most comfortable working? Who are your most comfortable co-workers or bosses? Describe your current situation as this is our starting place.

2. Describe the absolute craziest thing you could ever imagine doing for a living. What would it be? A skydiving instructor? Taste-testing eclairs at a Swiss chocolate factory?

As you can see, there is a whole WORLD of room between answer #1 and #2, and the willingness to explore just a little of that territory will show you all the ways that stepping out of your comfort zone can expand your career.

Strengthening Your Imagination

Growing a stronger imagination is a vital skill in creating a better future, both individually and collectively. Ruha Benjamin, a Professor of Sociology at Boston University, says, "What we are fighting for is our imagination, the right to imagine a life and relationships and a social world that are happier, less anxious, more harmonious and more just. We are not being diligent enough or deliberate enough about cultivating our imagination. We have to fight for our ability to imagine the world we want."

As any fiction writer will tell you, having a stronger imagination does NOT require you to loosen your grip on reality or truth. If we cannot imagine a better future, then it is almost impossible to create one.

1. When you were 15 what kind of work or job or career did you imagine you would be doing right now at this age? What kind of adulthood did you imagine for yourself?

2. Take a minute to remember the worst job you ever had in your whole life, at any age. What were you doing? Imagine three things that COULD have happened but did not, (no matter how wildly you must imagine!) that would have made that job more bearable.

-
-
-

3. Imagine the next year of your life and some of the changes you might make in your career. Write a list of ten statements. Start each statement with the words "What if" and be as specific as you can. For example, instead of just writing "What if I worked less?" try being more specific and consider, "What if I worked six hours on Mon and Tues and took Sundays completely off to spend with family?" Do not be afraid to come up with some ideas that feel radical!

    - What if

    - What if

    - What if

    - What if

    - What if

    - What if

    - What if

    - What if

    - What if

- What if

4. Imagine the best thing that could possibly happen in your current job or job search. What would it feel like if that thing happened? How would it feel to really fly? How would it help your personal and professional self-esteem or self-worth?

5. Image a positive and strong image of yourself at the age of retirement or voluntarily leaving the work world. What does that look like? How old will you be? Where will you be living? What will you do with your time and energy when working is no longer a requirement? What will you be passionate about?

Storms, Roadblocks and Failure

Every life is filled with people, places, situations, and circumstances that rise up to block our path forward. We have an incredible human ability to work through these roadblocks and come out on the other side with a renewed passion, purpose, and determination to succeed.

1. In the "The Wizard of Oz" a tornado takes Dorothy to a scary place and she desperately tries to get back home. How have you dealt with these troubling storms in your life?

2. Dorothy goes through a lot of challenges, but her friends come to mean everything to her. Who are some of the people you met or people you created a deeper relationship with as a result of that storm? How have they contributed to your growth and expansion of self?

3. When you have wanted to try something NEW in your life or in your career, what have your biggest roadblocks been? Time? Money? Support? Fear of failure? Fear of success?

4. When you have failed at something work-related in the past, how did you handle that failure? Were you angry? Depressed? Determined?

5. Have you ever witnessed someone who handled failure or adversity in a way you respected or envied? Who were they? What did they fail at? How did they handle it?

6. Failure, on any level, can often be a growth tool instead of a death sentence. List three specific things your professional failures have taught you that you could not have learned any other way.

-
-
-

Exploring Your Relationship With Fear

Fear and uncertainty, trepidation, and worry, are all very normal human emotions and all are activated in response to different circumstances in our lives. For those seeking to reinvent their career and rediscover their true goals and passions, fear can be like a dragon lurking deep within us, holding us back from what we really want. It can keep us from growing and developing in ways that will uplift our lives. So how do we fight the fear and do what needs to be done? We ask better questions and align our goals with the answers we find.

Lots of hard-working people are afraid to fail in their career. When we fail it brings us closer to learning who we really are and what matters most to us. Fear has a way of making us focus only on what could go wrong while losing sight of what could go right. Many times, in the recruiting world, I encounter those who are afraid to apply for a new position or afraid to shift their career goals or ask a boss for a raise. I am amazed by those who FEEL that fear and then roll up their sleeves and do it anyway! Working with fear is a relationship and pushing through what scares us can strengthen our self-confidence and self-esteem.

1. Describe a time in your work life when you were afraid. What was the worst-case scenario?

Times When You Have Been FORCED to Adapt and Change

1. Make a list of five unexpected events in your career that affected you personally. What adversity did you have to overcome to survive and adapt? Perhaps the company you worked for went through downsizing, consolidated job duties, adopted new technology, required new certifications, etc. Be as specific as you can.

    -
    -
    -
    -
    -

2. Choose one of those events in the list above in which you had to adapt and create a new normal. Describe it in detail. What happened?

3. What lessons did you learn from this adaptation? How did you grow or change as a person?

Calculated Risk

Being wary or afraid of change is a normal feeling especially in a work world where we are afraid to make a mistake and possibly lose what we have in the search for something better. A big part of my career as a recruiter is helping people determine when it is TIME to make a change or seek a better position. Change is powerful and strengthening our ability to change our lives is an incredible skill to have.

Change is not always reckless or dangerous and the key is to understand the nature of calculated risk, a risk in which we work to understand all the possible outcomes as much as we can. Calculated risks, big or small, allow us to grow and expand. They are chances for us to take a new journey into who we have the capacity to become. They allow us to surprise ourselves. How have calculated risks in your life contributed to who you are today?

1. Describe a time in your life when you took a calculated risk. Did you take a risk in college on a new class that proved to be a rewarding experience? Did you take a trip or vacation to a new place that opened horizons for you and forever changed your outlook or disposition? How did it feel? How did you grow or change?

2. Describe a calculated risk you have taken in your work life. What was the risk? What was the outcome?

A New Mindset: Review, Reconsider, Restart

Stepping Out of Our Comfort Zone can be an opportunity for a new growth mindset, changing our lives in ways we never thought possible. A friend of mine reminded me of the "Moss Rose." In some cultures, this rose is considered a weed because it can take over a garden. In other cultures, it is highly desired for its beauty and fragrance. It really depends on the gardener's perspective. Let your perspective have an expanded growth mindset and step out of your comfort zone into the New Work World that might offer benefits you could only have imagined.

The idea of becoming aware of the subjectivity of our perceptions is an admittedly abstract one, the likes of which are considered philosophy and science fiction. However, human perceptions and their ramifications are very real and potentially life changing. Research shows that people may hold an unconscious bias against creativity because it represents uncertainty unless they are able to perceive that uncertainty in a positive light.

Author Amanda Enayati once wrote, "Consider the role perception plays in helping patients improve in ailments ranging from pain and depression to Parkinson's disease through the phenomenon known as the placebo effect. Though the placebo effect remains largely shrouded in mystery, researchers attribute some aspects of the placebo response to active mechanisms in the brain that can influence bodily processes such as the immune response and release of hormones."

We read so much these days about "changing mindset" and I think it is critical for our own sanity that we change our way of thinking. We must change our perception because when we do the gates of our mind can open to innovation and transformation. Our minds are much more powerful than we think, and we often do not give them enough credit. We can create a positive environment by focusing upon positive thoughts and affirmations. We are what we think.

How might we harness the power of perception to live more deliberate lives and perhaps even recast the most challenging situations, like this pandemic, and the effects of it in the New Work World that we find ourselves living in?

Being a very "pragmatic" individual, as someone recently described me, this process of Stepping Out of My Comfort Zone and changing my own mindset is not really an easy process. Could I be trying to make Fiction out of Reality? A big smile came to my face as I remembered my loving father's wise counsel when he taught me the power of perception and imagination to create the reality I wanted. He would often say, "If you keep telling yourself you can't achieve this or that, you won't. If you put your mind to it, you can achieve whatever it is you want in life." I have never forgotten his wise words.

One way to expand your mindset is to practice these three steps:

1. REVIEW

Do a thorough review of where you have been in your career and what is reasonably available to you now. Believe in yourself and that you have what it takes to navigate rough waters. Research your current options and do what is necessary to establish a plan of action. If you need to take more online classes to become more familiar with the digital world, do it. If you need to take a bit of a pay cut for now to put food on the table, evaluate what there is in your current lifestyle you can do without. It must start with YOU and the mindset that you will survive these challenging times and be able to communicate your service orientation and strong contribution to a prospective employer.

What are some initial tasks you would be willing to do from the list above in conducting a Review of your abilities and possibilities?

-
-
-
-
-

2. RECONSIDER

In this step you Reconsider how you can refine your skill set to meet the demands of the New Work World. If there is more of a need for temporary or contract workers at this time, investigate the opportunities and if perhaps those jobs might eventually go permanent. Reconsider how you may have to take two part-time jobs to maintain your financial balance at this time and realize that this will not last forever. Understand that you are not stagnant. You are not stuck with the amount of talent or competency you were born with. Realize you can choose to expand your skill set with deliberate action and determination to expand and grow. You are the only one navigating your boat to calmer waters ahead. You will get there with the right compass and strategic plan. First, you must believe in yourself and your abilities that you can do it and change your mindset to be able to get to this new destination.

What are some initial tasks you would be willing to do from the list above in Reconsidering how you might move forward?

-
-
-
-
-

3. RESTART

If you have taken a risk or tried something new, if you have failed at something or lost a job or been downsized, do not look at this situation as an ending. Consider it as a new beginning to allow you to meet many interesting people along the way and contribute to your own personal growth and expanded awareness of your work world journey. Just because you have been, for example, a sales assistant in the oil and gas business, doesn't mean those skills are not transferable into another industry that uses the same skill set mechanics of tracking, logistics, follow-up and back-up to the sales force. It might have to be done now in more of an online/digital way with less face-to-face interaction. The online jobs of the future will allow us to have more interface with people and cultures in different countries that might add value and enhance our understanding of the job and the world at large.

What are some initial tasks you would be willing to do to Reset and Restart your new career path from exactly where you are now?

-
-
-
-

Coming Home to Who You Really Are

Even surviving our darkest days allow us to dig deep within ourselves, to examine our goals and passions, and these times might allow us to really shine in exciting ways. If we slay that inner Dragon of fear and self-doubt and move through our limiting beliefs and roadblocks, amazing illumination can take place. Many famous people, including Shakespeare, Sir Isaac Newton and even Levi Straus, and many other great inventors and industrial revolutionists, have used dark times to make major inventions and breakthroughs that we hold dear today. Historically, self-knowledge and innovation have driven changes beneficial to workers and humanity at large while new workplace trends hold the promise of greater productivity that will fuel broader well-being.

1. What does "Coming Home to Who You Really Are" mean to you?

2. How do you imagine your life and career might be different if you were more in alignment with your true gifts, values, and talents?

Stepping Out of Your Comfort Zone is one of the key elements to success. You have to be willing to try something different and walk through your fear; whatever that fear might be. When you are willing to use your imagination and take a chance on yourself, you raise your chances of success exponentially.

CHAPTER 4

TAKING THE TIME TO DO IT RIGHT

The great thinkers and scholars throughout the ages have all had their say about how much time it really takes to do something right. Ben Franklin said, "Take time for all things: great haste makes great waste." William Shakespeare said, "Wisely and slow, they stumble that run fast." There is a Chinese Proverb that says, "Be not afraid of growing slowly, be afraid only of standing still." Even the late great comedian Robin Williams said, "Why do they call it Rush Hour when nothing moves?"

I think that, from all these quotes above the central idea is quite clear. If we rush the process, we go nowhere. Taking the time to do it right is necessary if we want to reach a meaningful goal of any type, whether it be personal or professional. With the possible exception of love at first sight, nothing worthwhile happens in a heartbeat!

Taking Your Time

1. Think of three times in your personal life when you took your time to do something right. What comes to mind? What did you do? Where were you? Were you painting the living room? Teaching a child to ride a bike? Building a website? Was it a class you took that you really prepared well for every week and studied hard and got a good grade? Was it a relationship that started off as friendship and grew into a strong love because you took the time to build a solid foundation? List them here:

    •

    •

-

2. How might these same accomplishments have been completely different if you had rushed your way through it? How would the outcome for each one be different?

   -
   -
   -

3. Think of three times in your work life when you took your time to get a better outcome or more success. Was it choosing to get additional training or certifications? Was it a time when you took on extra projects and received a promotion or salary increase because of your careful planning? List them here:

   -
   -
   -

Rushing Through It

Often when we try to rush GREATNESS, it does not turn out to our advantage, and something we do not always learn until we give it a try. As the old saying goes, "Rome wasn't built in a day!"

1. Think of a time when you tried to rush the process of something important in your personal life. What did you try to rush through? Changing a flat tire in the rain? Cramming the night before a big exam and then getting a low grade? Think of a time you did not prepare well for something in your personal or family life and the end result was a disaster. Describe that experience here:

2. Think of a time when you rushed through something in your work life. Did you say yes to the wrong job too quickly? Did you ever jump into a new job where you were not fully prepared or did not have the correct credentials? Did you lose the job or get a poor performance review? Maybe it was a time when you really wanted to appear to others as if you had that gold medal accomplishment but you found out in the process that it took much more work than you ever imagined. Did you ever speed through a project for work and miss some critical steps in the process? Describe what happened here:

Planning and Goal Setting

The ability to make plans, manage time, set goals and see them through to completion are vitally important skills for anyone serious about growing and expanding their career into greater levels of success and accomplishment. These are not skills we are born with; we learn them along the way.

1. Describe three times in your life when you deliberately set out a plan of action or set up a goal and, because you had a plan, a road map, you were able to achieve your target.

    •

    •

    •

2. How did you feel when you achieved these goals successfully?

3. We all fly by the seat of our pants sometimes. How does having a method or system in place help you when striving towards a goal?

4. What advice would you give to a friend or co-worker who is against planning and goal setting?

5. Name three important goals you are setting for yourself in your personal life right now. What do you want to do? Pay off your mortgage? Learn to speak Italian? Spend more time with your family?

-
-
-

6. For each of those three goals, think of the time frame you have set to achieve each one. Is the time frame realistic? Is it too short? Too long? Are there measurable markers along the way? Make some notes on those time frames for each goal here:

-
-
-

7. Do the same thing for three professional/career goals you have right now. What goals have you set for yourself and what will it take to get you there? Under each goal make some notes about the timeline of how much time you estimate it might take to achieve that goal.

-
-
-

Training Towards Excellence

There are many careers, job paths, educational designations, etc., that take years to accomplish. It could be becoming a doctor, lawyer, Ph.D., architect, designer, engineer, etc. Think about the benefits that go along with these types of prestigious and high-end careers. People who commit to training in these fields undergo years of hard work, both in school and in the workplace, and they meet many interesting people and colleagues along the way.

Even if we are not called to work in those specialty areas we often need more or specialized training to get to where we want to go. We might need to go back to school, take on-line courses, get a certification to improve our skills or even join professional groups like Toastmasters or the Rotary Club. There are many reputable on-line and virtual sources for training and skill building as well as peer groups and coaching opportunities.

1. Name some of the training or skill-building experiences you have had, in or out of school, that have been the most valuable to you?

   -
   -
   -

2. What are you willing to research or try? What types of training could truly help you achieve your goals and make you stand out in a crowd? What would be worth the investment of time, money, and effort into expanding our knowledge/experience base? How are you willing to expand all facets of self?

   -
   -
   -

Getting the Support We Need to Succeed

No one achieves big career goals totally alone. We are always working with and around other people in our personal and professional lives. It is ok to ask for help or support as you work your way towards the career goals you have set for yourself? Often the effort and time we invest in building and maintaining support systems and friendships can also contribute in huge ways to our sense of balance, well-being and to our personal growth. If we have an important goal but feel a real lack of support in attaining it, we need to investigate the measures we might take to make it happen.

1. Look at the three major career goals you listed above. What kind of support from family, friends, co-workers etc., do you need to have the support necessary to achieve each of these goals?

    •

    •

    •

    •

2. Having support from peers and friends is helpful, but sometimes we also need support from professionals or mentors trained to help us achieve our goals. Would a career coach, a mentor, a therapist, a trainer, or any other professional help move you past the fear of achieving your goal? Often a minister/pastor/priest of a religious affiliation can be a possible source of support if funds are tight and we really need someone to talk to. Would someone like that be useful to you?

   There is a lot of value in using a mentor or getting advice when we are making major decisions connecting our happiness with our livelihood. Discussing goals and ideas with a mentor can help us see more clearly if our goals or timelines are reasonable and if they will offer solid returns for our investment and effort? Could you connect with someone on LinkedIn or social media to discuss the benefits/roadblocks in your goals or new career path? Make a list of four possible professional sources you might be willing to seek support in achieving your career goals.

   -
   -
   -
   -

When we create a map for ourselves and take the time to do it right, we find ourselves in a better position to make the most of the opportunities at hand.

CHAPTER 5

BE A HUNTER

The Fifth Step of the Faremouth Method, Be a Hunter, was born out of the many employer requests I have received through the years as a recruiter to find "Hunter" type candidates as opposed to "Gatherers."

The word "hunter" means different things to different people, but as human beings we are all hunting and searching for something. The kind of "hunting" I am referring to here is not simply hunting as a sport but hunting as a mindset. Being a hunter means going after what we want in the work world instead of expecting or waiting for it to simply come to us.

Humans have been engaged in hunting and gathering for as long as we have been on earth. Both practices are intrinsic to fulfilling our basic human needs. The original caveman foraged for his food and his survival in whatever ways were at his disposal. The "Hunters" were those who went out and killed the animal for food and then brought it home to the "Gatherers" who essentially performed less aggressive tasks in preparing the food for distribution. Even now in the modern world, the hunter's instinct to go out and get what we need to survive is still a vital part of our human DNA. In the business world, what we gather and what we hunt have everything to do with our success and reaching our career goals.

The Hunter's Mindset

A positive and optimistic Mindset can make a tremendous difference in how we plan to reach our goals. When we believe in ourselves and recognize what we are capable of achieving, we have a much better ability to manifest exactly what we want with deliberate and focused strategic planning.

1. List five things that you currently do to create a positive and optimistic mindset, especially about your potential, your work and your career.

    -
    -
    -
    -
    -

2. List five things that you could implement into your daily routine to make a difference in your life and create a MORE positive or self-confident mindset.

    -
    -
    -
    -
    -

3. Some jobs we have over the course of our career take on more of the "Gatherer" qualities and others take on more "Hunter" qualities. For example, a Sales Assistant might be considered to be more of a "Gatherer" as opposed to an Outside Sales Representative who might be viewed as more of a "Hunter." List three jobs or work-related tasks or responsibilities you have had that felt more to you like gathering. How have you been the "Gatherer?"

    •

    •

    •

4. List three jobs or work-related tasks or responsibilities you have had that feel more like hunting. How have you been the "Hunter?"

    •

    •

    •

5. Which roles or tasks did you enjoy the most or were the most comfortable for you? Which were the most bothersome? Write one word next to each task above about how you felt when you did that task? Which tasks did you feel most aligned with?

6. In your current job situation, list a few ways in which you could be more of a "Hunter" to be more successful?

    -
    -
    -
    -

7. If you are more of a "Gatherer" type of worker and enjoy a job with repetitive tasks, how could you slowly transform your way of doing work into more of a Hunter/go-getter/ innovator style?

Being a Leader

In the New Work World, we must become leaders who are the ones who overcome past negative work experiences and present insecurities to imagine new solutions. They seek out and fulfill goals that require the realization of their own true potential. They are not content simply to follow or meet the bare minimum of what is required or to simply maintain the status quo.

Hunters are the ones who are out front making the connections and finding the opportunities that allow them to achieve their highest goals.

1. What was your best Hunt? What was a time you got out front in your personal or professional life and took the LEAD and had a great result?

2. What was your worst hunt? Was there a time you tried to take the LEAD and it did not go according to plan? Were you hunting for a new relationship or a new job in the same old familiar places that produced the same old results?

3. What two lessons did you learn from that failed hunt?

Moving Past Failure and Fear

When we are met with challenges and obstacles in our life, there is a natural tendency to look for purpose and meaning. Why did these particular events happen in our life? Are we complacent to sit back and do nothing or do we have that inner drive and motivation to move through situations where we can transform?

Life is all about evolution. We are hard-wired to arise from those difficulties to become something better than who we have been in the past. How do we grow as human beings and have a positive effect upon our lives and the lives of others around us?

Hunters are designed to react and resolve through conflict. That means that, as a hunter, we have to address our fears of the unknown. We have to be able to move through our own anxieties of what might lie on the other side and act on courage to face the unknown.

A perfect example of the hunter is Will Hunting, the protagonist in the award-winning movie, Good Will Hunting. Beneath all of his insecurity stemming from childhood abuse was a brilliant mind. A genius in disguise. Through the story he was able to address his fears and confront his early trauma to allow his brilliant mind to surface.

Each of us has the ability to become a Hunter by addressing our own fears, insecurities and failures. We can engage that same spirit and passion to achieve our own goals and desires.

1. List three personal or work-related fears or anxieties you have had a hard time facing or moving past.

    •

    •

    •

2. Describe a time you faced a fear and became stronger because of it. This could be anything from learning to swim in the ocean as a kid to asking your boss for a raise.

3. What is your biggest hurdle, fear or obstacle to overcome in your current employment situation?

4. List three fears you feel that you might now be ready to face and overcome, especially in your career.

   -
   -
   -

Deciding What Is Most Necessary

It is part of our human nature to look for meaning in our lives and that is a key part of the hunter mindset. When things are moving along in a complacent mode, we are less likely to initiate change. When things become difficult, we look for how we can make life a more effective experience. When we become the Hunter we seek to improve our lives, but first we have to acknowledge what is most important to us, what we value the most and need to put first.

We are all searchers, but these days what we search for and how we search has changed. There is more emphasis now on financial security, family interactions, socializing with friends and business associates, as well as the care it takes to maintain our health and our ability to stay safe. Our necessities have changed. This shift in our society has made us far more introspective as we engage in soul-searching to look for a truer meaning to our life and legacy.

1. What five things are the most meaningful to you right now? Which five things give your life the greatest sense of value and purpose?

    •

    •

    •

    •

    •

2. Describe one of the things from the list above that gives your life meaning, which you have not engaged with fully enough over the past year or two. Which thing do you wish you engaged more or spent more time attending to?

Making Decisions and Going for It

The hunter mindset encourages you to be strategic, get focused on your goals, choose your most effective moment to act and then to act decisively.

1. What are the four biggest changes you need to make to find new employment in the New Work World? Is it a location change? Do you need to expand your skill set? Can you take online classes to further your hunt for new employment? Can you be mentored? Do you need to totally change your field of work?
   -
   -
   -
   -

2. If the needs of your family are a concern, what help do you need to remedy those family issues? List five things that would help you in this process.
   -
   -
   -
   -
   -

3. Describe a time in your personal or work life when you made a hard decision and then immediately WENT FOR IT. What happened?

Embracing Innovation

In our New Work World, we will have a labor market that rewards a very different kind of worker. In the past, the workers who had the most to gain were those who embraced one single career for their entire working life – in other words, the "gatherers." They were the employees that went into the office every day, did essentially the same task, took an hour for lunch and left at 5:00 pm. There was a lot of value and dignity in this type of career; it was the standard model for the American worker.

In this new future, the workers best able to surf the big waves will be more like the "hunters," those who enjoy being on the move, constantly looking for new opportunities, and ready to do whatever it takes to come out on top. This means if they have to learn new skills, move to another city, freelance on the side, and sometimes make ends meet by finding opportunities on platforms like Uber, Lyft, online call centers, skill-based or hands-on careers, etc. they will do it. You could say that hunters have more of an "entrepreneurial mindset" and will be the demand of employers in the future.

Being a hunter also means embracing innovation, trying new things and new ways of doing things. For some this will mean developing new technology or implementing some new discipline or routine. We can all find a way out of our comfort zone by embracing something new.

1. Since the onset of the COVID crisis have you sought out new EXTERNAL interests, distractions, pastimes or hobbies that inspire you? List a few of them here:
   •
   •
   •
   •
   •

2. Have you hunted for new INTERNAL ways to ground yourself or create a more positive mindset? This could be a Mindfulness Practice like Yoga or Meditation, Tai Chi, Tai Kwon Do, music, breathing techniques or physical

exercise. What things have allowed you to grow as a person or improve your state of being? List three things that have contributed to creating a more positive mindset.

-
-
-

3. One of the most vital and innovative skills for anyone seeking to restart, diversify or expand their career is to get clear about your transferrable skills. These are the passions, skills and abilities that will be useful in any job, specifically the areas in which you have the most ability and experience. Make a list of skills that you have that may be transferable to other careers or other jobs within your field.

-
-
-
-
-
-

4. Brainstorm some fields or industries that might welcome those transferrable skills. For example, if you have worked as a Buyer in Retail for ten years, would a purchasing job of another product be a transferrable skill you could use to find a job in a different industry?

-
-
-
-
-
-
-
-

5. List three ways you are willing to be adventurous and innovative in building a work life to carry you towards your next big career move. For example, if your current situation is bleak in finding a full-time job, would you be willing to use your skill set to perhaps find two part-time jobs or a seasonal job that would pay the bills?

   Could you take an online class to enhance your skill set? An evaluative tool would be Birkman International, Inc. at www.birkman.com

   -
   -
   -

Searching for More

When we have or experience something of value, we sometimes want more of it. What we want "more" of usually changes as we evolve as human beings and our "more" shifts in response to the significant life experiences we encounter.

Being a hunter means knowing where your hunger lives and coming to terms with what you want versus what you need. The quest for MORE can be compulsive and anxiety provoking or it can be focusing and clarifying.

1. At this stage in your PERSONAL life what do you want MORE of? More friendships, more love, more free time, more serenity, more nature? More material things? Do you want to feel MORE purposeful or useful or like you are doing more meaningful work in the world? Do you need to surround yourself with more positive people? What are some of the inner changes of your own identity that you would like to hunt for? List your top ten biggest MOREs here.

    •
    •
    •
    •
    •
    •
    •
    •
    •
    •

2. What about your PROFESSIONAL life? Think of your last few jobs. What did you experience that you want MORE of in your next job? More money? More days off, more success, more support from your boss, more training on technology? What are your top ten?

-
-
-
-
-
-
-
-
-
-

3. What do you need LESS of in your personal or work life? Less aloneness? Less isolation? Less noise? Less traveling for work? Less desk work? Do you need to be less critical of yourself?

-
-
-
-
-
-
-
-
-

Using the Campfire

In real life hunting experiences with family and friends, hunters often sit around a cozy, warm campfire in the evening. Stories are often shared in that circle of trust where individuals have a chance to bond and share in one another's failures and successes.

1. Have other people communicated with you about their own hunt for a better job or a more meaningful life? What have you learned from those "campfire stories" that have aided you in your own hunt? Just like the bonding attributes of a physical campfire, have you virtually engaged in conversations with people in similar situations or other countries to gather information? List three things you have learned by listening to the stories told by others who are also on the "hunt" for a better life.

    -
    -
    -

2. Hunting also involves connections from one's past. Think of someone you might know who is in a place where they might refer you for a position or know of an opening or who can help. Maybe it's someone you know who can suggest a place for you to apply for a job. List five people you might reach out to and expand your network and let people know what it is you are hunting for.

    -
    -
    -
    -
    -

3. It is never too soon to start imagining what you might say if you reached out to one of those people. Choose one person on the list above and write

the first five sentences of the email you might send to them, asking for their help or advice.

4. Our computers and screens are often the glowing lights of the modern campfire we gather around. With technology being "front and center" in the New Work World, how can we hunt for virtual exposure that might allow us to grow and expand? Hunts you could participate in and expand your focus might be online college classes, professional organizations, online writing classes, Toastmasters (to refine speaking ability for interviews and presentations), webinars, virtual seminars, or training seminars in your career field. List five people or groups of people connected in the virtual world who you might reach out to.

    •

    •

    •

    •

    •

How We Win Matters

There are many different ways to "win", whether we are trying to win the game or win the job or win the girl. Some win by cheating or taking shortcuts. Some win by trampling on others or avoiding responsibility or making others look bad in the hope it will make themselves look better. There are positive and ethical ways to win. Ways to land the job or close the deal while keeping your values and ethics intact.

Hunters are the ones who win through perseverance, dedication, innovation and hard work. Grace and humility are not just words. They are qualities that employers and co-workers will see in you and value.

1. What would you say are your four biggest WINS in your life?

    -
    -
    -
    -

2. Is there one of the wins above that you wish you had handled with more maturity or graciousness? Describe here what you wish you had done differently.

3. Describe a win or an achievement that seemed impossible, something you never thought you could accomplish, but you did anyway?

4. Which qualities of being a Hunter do you think helped you get that win?

You have undoubtedly collected a great deal of information by addressing these questions about being a "hunter". You should now have the information that will help you find the exact steps to take to integrate the Hunter mentality into your career reinvention journey. Use these insights to create a higher level of success in your life by taking more initiative as you draw Hunter opportunities towards yourself.

CHAPTER 6

CONCLUSION: THE HUMAN ELEMENT

Rediscovering Your Answers/Rediscovering Yourself

If you filled in all the answers as you worked through this book, then good for you! You did a lot of work! Now is the time to make yourself a cup of coffee and sit back, take some time, and read through everything you wrote in this workbook. This is your chance to truly rediscover yourself, your experiences and beliefs and what matters most to you in your job and career path. Finding a strategic path forward in your career begins with this self-witnessing, seeing exactly who you are, what you care about and what you want.

As you read, take some notes. Take your time, try not to rush through, even if what you are reading feels surprising or repetitive, embarrassing or uncomfortable. Doing this work needs to result in both insight and in actionable steps that lead you FORWARD into a better life and career.

When you are done reading take a moment to be AMAZED at all you have discovered! See if you can answer these assessment questions:

1. What were the four biggest or most valuable things you learned about yourself after reading over this workbook:
   -
   -
   -
   -
2. What were the two biggest surprises?

-
-

3. Transferrable skills are a huge contemporary driving force in the New Work World. What skills, abilities, strengths, and passions did you discover that you have, that would serve you well in ANY industry or field, not just the one in which you are currently working? This should now be a BIGGER list than the one you made in Chapter Five! List them here:

-
-
-
-
-
-
-
-
-

4. Was there any way in which learning this revealed information about yourself that might change or refine your current job search or career path? What are you now willing to do? Describe it here:

These Action Tasks can be further strategized by working with a career consultant or employment coach. As an executive career consultant THIS is the work I do with clients every day!

A Vision to Move Towards

Often, we strive to "be happier" or "have a better life" without really asking deeper questions about what that truly looks like. This is your chance to move from this new awareness of your values and beliefs into creating a real vision for what that better life would look like, and the role that your career might play in building that life.

1. If you had a magic wand and could wave that wand and be anything you wanted to be, what would that look like?

2. Do you enjoy getting up in the morning and going into work? What would a perfect morning of getting up and going to your perfect job look like? How would you feel?

Re-read the answers to these questions often as you take your new steps in your new career. We often forget that we already hold the vision that we are moving towards.

Living Your Truth

Your "truth" is, of course, a big and abstract concept and it is different and unique for each of us. After filling out this whole workbook, how would you now define your personal Truth? What is most important to you in all the world? What do you hold to be most true? Describe it here:

What are some of the things that have prevented you from living your truth?

-
-
-
-
-

Often insight brings a new readiness to change. Based on where you are now, what are five things you are READY to do to jumpstart your job and career?

-
-
-
-
-

Putting it Into Action

Becoming our best self is a life-long process, and that journey is filled with many twists and turns along the way. Those of you who have had your work and home lives jump the tracks in the COVID pandemic know this better than most. So often during our life, we are ruled by a fear of failure, disappointment, facing rejection, etc. Adversity has a way of testing us as it is only when our lives become challenging that we see how strong we truly are.

When we go through tough times, I always recall the famous quote by Henry Ford, "When everything seems to be going against you, remember that the airplane takes off against the wind, not with it."

The work world will eventually evolve to a "new normal" and, when it does, you need to do all you can to be able to compete in this post-pandemic world. In the New Work World, if you are serious about securing a job or making a career shift, you will have to "put the pedal to the metal" to really be proactive and make a strong commitment to be able to stand out above the competition. The real winners are those who have resilience and perseverance. You really do have choices as to how you respond and dedicate your energies to create new opportunities for yourself.

Your new prospective employer will not tolerate why your resume has formatting issues, why your references won't return a call, why your LinkedIn profile is not up-to-date and professional, why you have been too stressed out with fear of Covid-19, family, kids, etc. These issues and attitudes could very well cost you the job offer later.

Doing this work now will allow you to look more appealing than the candidate who might have more experience than you do, but who DID NOT prepare or put his self-knowledge into ACTION. Employers always look for a candidate with that something extra as they determine the best applicant for the job. It is important to remember that not only are you, the applicant, going through a new learning curve on how to approach securing a new job, so are companies and employers.

Now that you have done a realistic self-analysis to document your skills and weaknesses, you are ready to strategize how to secure a new career.

Here is a checklist of specific tasks that will help you enter or re-enter the job market from a strong foundation and make you stand out above the rest. Take your notes from your work in this workbook and keep them close by as you follow the checklist below.

Checklist for Getting Ready for Your Next Job

1. Do research to target a new job or industry that would be more profitable and secure than the one you currently have or came from.

2. If you are NOT currently unemployed then contact your previous bosses to secure reference letters. Inform them that a possible prospective employer might be calling and express gratitude for them taking the time out of their day to answer any questions about your previous work performance.

3. Assume that you might be asked by a new employer why you were laid off, terminated or furloughed in this pandemic; how would you explain? Remember to express gratitude for the experience and reserve any hard feelings about the loss of your unemployment. Omit any negative talk about a particular industry, boss or co-worker. Get very clear and realistic about your compensation goals.

4. Analyze your monthly household living expenses to see if there are ways to cut back so that you are not working for just a paycheck.

5. If you want to find employment that is going to satisfy your passions and utilize your skills then it might be worth taking a step back in order to take a giant step forward. Have you examined your realistic worth based on your experience, training, and employment history in the current marketplace? What other fields are you willing to work in, as well as your own? Do some research on this.

6. Clean up ALL of your social media content. This is more important than you might imagine. This means Twitter, Facebook, Instagram, TikTok, Pinterest, YouTube, everything you use. Make sure your content does not contain anything inappropriate, embarrassing or unprofessional. This might be pictures with you holding an alcoholic beverage, wearing revealing clothing or posts that include inappropriate language that might be offensive to a prospective employer, etc. As a recruiter, I have heard clients tell me that they did look at a prospective employee's Facebook account and decided to pass on making an offer, even if they were the top candidate, because of what the social media profile demonstrated

that was not in alignment with their company values and principles. Remember to clean up your LinkedIn profile and make sure it has current and contemporary information. Make sure everything about you reflects a professional, honest, and highly motivated individual.

7. Practice Self-Care and lean on your trusted community members for support. Find a trusted mentor, friend, previous boss, or family member who you can lean on for support if the stress of your job search becomes overwhelming.

8. Consider trying mindfulness techniques such as Yoga, meditation, prayer, or visualization to help you get centered and calm down during this process of seeking new employment in the New Work World.

9. Have some fun and make time to exercise, relax and involve yourself in hobbies that you might enjoy. If it's not possible to get to a gym or health club, what other exercise or movement could you do to assist you with high stress? Could spending more of your free time outdoors in nature be a soothing remedy for your fears about your future?

10. Keep taking notes for yourself to track your thoughts, feelings, goals, insights and all the information you find on your search for the career and job you really want!

This transformational time can be used as a very important step by re-introducing ourselves to the New Work World. The more in touch you are with your true self, the more you will have to offer and the more power you will have to make the world a better place. In the process, we may find that our new life is better than the one we left behind.

The Human Element and the Importance of Giving Back

The Five Step Faremouth Method is a method whose effectiveness has been proven over many different individuals and industries for decades. It really does have far reaching ramifications. The core of The Faremouth Method is not simply self-awareness or a shift in our own mindset, it is the willingness to USE these things to give back to the world we live in. That, for me, is always the Greater Good. So how can we give back? Giving back means using your own strengths and abundances to support and help those who have a greater level of need. It means leaving the world a better place than we found it. As many business leaders have been demonstrating in many different fields and industries, it is also good business. Would the time and effort be worth it to you if you were able to create or offer something, no matter how small, that would really contribute to the greater good or society?

We do not all have to be billionaires with money to burn in order to make the world a better place. As difficult as the year 2020 was, we saw time and time again how simple human decency and kindness allowed people to give whatever they had, to whomever needed it the most. When we support our friends and neighbors and extend compassion and generosity to others, we build a stronger society. We literally create the conditions for people to be happier which means a better world where people who are happy and feel respected and valued in their workplace report less illness, higher job satisfaction and greater productivity and innovation. This leads to higher rates of retention and a better societal environment for us all.

A new process for employment is being birthed for all parties concerned. This is a time where the HUMAN ELEMENT of recruiting, employment and finding a new career can be best served by the recruiter's detective skills sleuthing out the hidden talents of the potential employee and how these talents might match perfectly with a potential employer. You might be surprised at how much giving back could support your own goals. How could trying something as simple as volunteering on a weekend provide a valuable insight to a new career path?

1. What are some of the ways YOU want to "give back" to your industry, your community or your society?

-
-
-
-
-

2. What are a few things that would make it EASIER for you to begin to give more back to those around you?

-
-
-
-
-

Simple Steps with Profound Results

Recruiting has always been and always will be about the Human Element. It is NOT simply the business of matching resumes to job listings. It is the much more profound business of matching people to communities. I believe that the Human Element is now even more important in the New Work World than it has ever been.

My five-step method was developed to help others streamline the process in their career journey to avoid serious detrimental consequences. The Human Element is now center stage for all of us to see. In times of great challenge, we always see both the best and the worst sides of human nature on full display. Lately we have seen a huge eruption of altruism and working together, doctors and nurses risking their lives on the front lines, neighbors collecting food and running errands for one another, volunteers sewing masks, restaurant owners using some of the food on hand to bring to the nearest shelter, etc.

This is an example of how there is always HOPE for a better world, regardless of how dire our circumstances might be. Historians tell us that a crisis can be a turning point for societies. Just like how workers had to reinvent themselves after the Great Depression, this crisis, too, could lead to something better. As workers we can now bridge our differences in the workplace as opposed to wanting to be looked at for our unique experience or generational category. Maybe the era of Boomers vs. Millennials and competition between the two could come to an end and we might just inaugurate a new age of solidarity and connection.

That famous saying by Mother Teresa really makes sense right now. "You know what I don't know, I know what you don't know, but together we can do great things." Our unique ability to work together and move from a critical to a more hopeful view of humanity is our true mission and goal. No matter who we are, our purpose and objective is very much aligned. Our focus is to contribute to our work world and allow us all to bring out the best in ourselves and in each other.

I do not think we will ever go back to the "normal" as we knew it, but rather to a "new normal" that will foster much more collaboration and teamwork. It will be a series of simple and steady steps, both individually and collectively, that will get us there.

A New Mindset for the New Work World

As a candidate for a position, when you are interviewing with prospective employers you will now have to (to paraphrase President Kennedy) not just ask what a company can do for YOU but be clear about what you can do for THEM. All candidates in this New Work World are going to have to hold onto a healthy sense of self-esteem while getting rid of any entitled attitudes they might be holding. We will have to shift our expectations away from WHAT WE THINK

WE ARE OWED and more towards WHAT WE CAN CONTRIBUTE.

With 30 million people on unemployment at the time of this writing, it's for sure going to be what we call an "Employer's Market" and employers are going to have the "pick of the litter" as they say. What will also matter will be strategy and how our skill set will contribute in a grand way to the bottom line of the company. The mindset of "well boss, that wasn't in the job description when I interviewed for this job" is not going to serve the candidate of the future well in this New Work World. We are going to see more teamwork and requirements to do more than we were hired for in the jobs of the future.

A renewed sense of HOPE, a NEW Normal, and a big change in the attitudes and mindsets of employees will be the three areas that we can look forward to in our New Work World. This pandemic may have allowed us to implement more harmonious and productive efforts in our workplace that might be a move away from competition and greed and a move toward more positive interactions that will have a win-win for all going forward.

Out of crisis comes opportunity. We all have the potential to turn this world crisis into a golden opportunity. As we change our mindsets from what we knew before and embrace that new caliber of the future, we can create a bigger, better world not only in our workplace but also in our personal relationships and families. We have already seen a much broader coming together and how it takes a team to work together to create strategies that benefit all.

This is the time to develop new skills, not only to help us do our job but also to develop new interpersonal skills and how we deal with others. We have an opportunity now to learn more about how to deal with conflict and challenge in our new workspaces. We may be going back into an area similar to where we had been but even that is now changed. We might find more division is required between us and a coworker in our physical workspace. It is inherent that we will automatically fall into these new working patterns as we return to employment. It will be so important to develop strong teams in order to accomplish the job in front of us.

Coming Home

Don't we all want to come home to who we truly are? Coming home is a process we go through our entire life. The "home" I am referring to here is in a more metaphorical sense. It relates to that inner peace and internal home of joy and comfort we all are seeking. Whether it is during good times or bad, I think we all can find comfort coming home to a place of peace and tranquility inside ourselves. There is a lot of attention these days about "mindfulness" or changing mindset practices to assist us in this process, especially in times of upheaval and uncertainty.

By seeking out new experiences and working through change and conflict, we discover our true self which is similar to getting ourselves into alignment or being true to who we are. At different stages of our lives, and through sometimes challenging experiences, we are forced to re-evaluate and reinvent ourselves to get into that alignment of our true purpose and life goals. The famous author, Maxwell Maltz, says it like this:

"Creative striving for a goal that is important to you as a result of your own deep-felt needs, aspirations and talents, brings happiness as well as success because you will be functioning as you were meant to function. Man is by nature a goal-striving being. And because man is "built that way" he is not happy unless he is functioning as he was made to function as a goal-striver. Thus, success and true happiness not only go together but each enhances the other. Creativity also leads to a longer life. Many creative people produce their greatest works during their senior years. It may also explain why some men die soon after they retire. They no longer have a creative/productive outlet."

Your willingness to answer the questions in this workbook shows that you are on a journey of self-discovery to find your way home to who you really are. This is how we reinvent ourselves during uncertain times. The information you have collected here can help you transfer your skills into another area if you have fear of losing your job, or if you have already been a part of a layoff or on a furlough. What if we have lost our job, a spouse, life as we have known it? What is the constant that can keep us going? Can keep us from falling apart? Can allow us to be like a huge oak tree with its deep roots in the ground?

The only constant in our lives is change. Being in alignment in our 20's might look very different from being in alignment in our 40's and beyond. Yet there is always a way to reach our destination to allow our creativity to flourish and bring us the happiness we seek.

Sometimes our journey to get back home is filled with many roadblocks. If we let our internal determination and "compass" direct our path, and not let external events dictate our journey, we can emerge stronger, happier beings through the process.

The key is to change our mindset and realize that our instinct and humanity always knows the way back home and will get us there. No matter what happens we know our core beliefs will always help us achieve our goals. Keep the information you gathered in exploring this Five Step Method close to you as you roll up your sleeves to reinvent your life and career. It will help you learn to value and deepen your relationship with who you truly are and what you truly want, and that is the internal compass that we must learn to trust. It will always lead us on the path home.

ACKNOWLEDGMENTS

I have been blessed in my life to have so many people to thank for their assistance in bringing this project to life: my Content/Developmental Editor, Max Regan; my Layout and Cover Designer, Mark Gelotte; my dear friend and Line Editor/Proofreader, Marva Mason; Ron Bueker, my Web Designer, and Russ Riddle, my attorney.

I am grateful to my two sons, Daniel and Christopher Sandland, as well as the rest of my family for their love and support. My thanks to my close friends and my wonderful team: Natalia, Suzanna, Bobbie, Susan, Kathy, Don, Svetlana, Fern and Sandi. A thank you to all of my many recruiting clients, candidates and associate recruiter network friends for their contribution of real-life information and data. A special thanks to the professional organizations that have encouraged me to write this book for industry information and guidance in the New Work World, including: NASPD, NAPCA, Mensa, District 56 Toastmasters, Authors Marketing Guild, Houston Writers Guild and the Non-fiction Author Association, as well as Kevin Price and Cindy Sharp at the Price of Business Show. Thanks also to Houston Community College, University of Houston, St. Thomas University, Texas A&M and Sam Houston State University for allowing me to teach and speak about the value of reinvention.

As always, to Brodie and Hunter, who showed so much affection throughout the creation of this book.

REFERENCES

Amanda, Enayati. 2016. *Seeking Serenity*. Gildan Media LLC.

Hill, Napoleon. 2012. *Think and Grow Rich*. New York: Start Publishing. Kindle edition.

Leopold, Till Alexander, Vesselina Ratcheva, and Saadia Zahidi. January 2016. *The Future of Jobs: Employment, Skills and Workforce Strategy for the Fourth Industrial Revolution*. Geneva: World Economic Forum. Accessed February 8, 2017. http://www3.weforum. org/docs/WEF_Future_of_Jobs.pdf.

Marshall, Tess. 2011. "21 Tips to Release Self-Neglect and Love Yourself in Action." *Tiny Buddha: Simple Wisdom for Complex Lives*. http://tinybuddha.com/blog/21-tips-to-release-self-neglect-and-love-yourself-in-action/.

Maxwell, Maltz. 2015. *Psycho-Cybernetics: Updated and Expanded*. TarcherPerigee; Updated, Expanded ed. edition

"MBTI Basics," The Myers & Briggs Foundation, accessed February 7, 2017, http://www.myersbriggs.org/my-mbti-personality-type/mbti-basics.

McLeod, Saul. 2007 (updated 2016). "Maslow's Hierarchy of Needs." *Simply Psychology*. http://www.simplypsychology.org/maslow.html.

PwC. 2014. *17th Annual Global CEO Survey, 2014: US Report*. London: PricewaterhouseCoopers. Accessed February 8, 2017. http://www. pwc. com/us/en/ceo-survey-us/2014/assets/2014-us-ceo-survey.pdf.

Wayne, Dyer. 2004. *The Power Of Intention: Change The Way You Look At Things And The Things You Look At Will Change*. Hay House UK.

Mary Ann Faremouth is the founder and CEO of Faremouth & Company and a highly regarded recruiter, career consultant, speaker and writer. She has been a placement specialist and a leader in the national recruiting community and has placed thousands of employees since 1982. She was the 2016 President of the Houston Independent Personnel Consultant Group and is a board member of the NASPD (National Association of Steel Pipe Distributors) and Authors Marketing Guild. She specializes in recruitment of professional, clerical, and temporary placements, with a variety of industry specific positions in various fields. Her expertise is in matching quality applicants with the right job, serving companies ranging from thriving independents to global conglomerates, tailoring each engagement to the client's needs.

Mary Ann holds a CPC (Certified Personnel Consultant) credential, is certified by the Board of Regents of the National Association of Personnel Consultants in Washington, D.C., and was awarded an Advanced Communicator Bronze, Advanced Leader Bronze Awards by Toastmasters. She cofounded *Jobs: Houston* magazine in 1997. Mary Ann maintains affiliations with professional organizations in various other industries, including oil and gas, financial, construction, IT, and structural, mechanical, and civil engineering. She has a keen understanding of the marketplace and its specialized needs and requirements.

Mary Ann brings a wealth of expertise to clients looking for the right individual to maximize and empower their team. As a consultant she is available to assist both the applicant and the client to quickly adapt to the New Work World.

She also offers virtual and in-person workshops to guide individuals through personalized self-discovery to find new career paths. She continues to build her affiliations with recognized leadership organizations to best serve her clients and applicants by creating a network of highly professional contacts throughout the world. She utilizes her platform as a writer and speaker through her articles and affiliations to reach those in need of help, offering hands-on guidance to navigate this uncharted territory (more information on www.faremouth.com).

Mary Ann's award-winning first book *Revolutionary Recruiting* has been listed by Book Authority as Number #1 of the Best 100 Recruiting Books; #1 Best Seller, Non-Fiction by Amazon (2019); Top 20 Recruiting books by Recruitics; Readers' Choice finalist (2019) by Houston Literary Awards; Best Non-Fiction (2018), Best Cover (2019), and Best Self-Help (2018) by Authors Marketing Guild. Her books support individuals and corporations, teaching them how to tap into each candidate's unrealized potential to find the right person for each job, maximizing both employee satisfaction as well as the employer's bottom line. Mary Ann also showcases her expertise of the recruiting world **on a monthly podcast for** *The Price of Business* **and weekly articles** for *USA Business Radio*. **Mary Ann lives in Houston, Texas.**

Made in the USA
Middletown, DE
23 December 2021

56225181R00060